Defeat/
No Surrender

Defeat/
No Surrender

COLIN GREER

ACMI PRESS
New York

ACMI Press, Inc.
351 East 84th Street, Ste. 10d, New York, NY 10028
www.acmipress.org
acmipress@gmail.com

Defeat/No Surrender

Copyright © 2023 by Colin Greer
Book Cover Design & Interior Layout by Dynamic Book Design

All rights reserved. No part of this work may be reproduced or utilized in any form or by any means, electronic or mechanical, including the internet, photocopying, microfilming, recording, or by an information storage and retrieval system, without permission in writing from the publisher.

978-1-883148-28-7 (Print)
978-1-883148-29-4 (Ebook)

Library of Congress Control Number: 2021940142

Dedication

To my dearest loving friend and teacher Jerry Epstein

Contents

Introduction
    Introduction 11
    Sonnet for Jerry 13

Part I: Salvation, by all means
    I Wish I Could Speak Yiddish Like Satchmo 16
    The Devil Has No Secrets 17
    Genesis 19
    Abiding 20
    Fly in Haman's Ointment 21
    The Impossible Is Possible 23
    Intoxication 25
    Improv 23
    Salvation, by all means 27
    Moved by a Mountain 28
    Self Improvement 29
    Today, Tomorrow 31

    Scarecrow Me 32
    Sabbath 33
    Freud 34
    Me Real/You Real 35
    Holiness 36
    False Witness 37
     (Heidegger's) They 39
    Who Can Stop Them 41
    Moses Rose Up 42
    Tarot 43
    Release 44
    Foil 46
    As Time Passes 47
    Essential 49
    A Chimp in the Mirror 52
    Meditation 53
    Such a Shame 54
    Contrition 56
    Imagining Heschel 57

Part II: Defeat/No Surrender
    Auntie, What's the Resistance? 60
    Swords into Plowshares 62
    Just a Thought 63
    Love in Quarantine 64
    One Eye of Jesus 65
    Emma Lazarus 67
    Fishers of Men 69

8 | Defeat/No Surrender

and the choir sings	71
The Ascent of Man	74
Hitchcock Through the Eyes of a Bird	76
Lady Macbeth Tells it Like it is	77
2 Cheers for the 1 Eyed Citizen	80
Patriot	83
The Sweet Shop Poem	85
Neighbors	87
What Is a Revolution	88
St. Augie	89
Ought Not Be But It Is	91
Unsettled Minds	92
Dixit	93
Oh My	94
Hand of the Sun	95
Up and Down	96
Defeat/No Surrender	97
When God Had No Name	101
Thou Shalt Not Stand Idly By	104
About the Author	107
About Dr. Jerry Epstein	108

Introduction

Dr. Jerry Epstein—"Jerry" as I called him—was a good good friend to many and a teacher to even more. Jerry pioneered a groundbreaking therapy to heal emotional and physical issues.

His teaching was subtle and quite direct. "Don't live in the future." "Don't be fearful, that's a future construct." "Why get all torn up about somewhere that does not exist?" "Why expend your life force like that?" "That goes for the past too—don't blame it, or anybody in it!" "The past does not exist." Yes! Yes! To life!

Jerry passed in 2019. Although he taught me to stay grounded in the present, when it comes to deep friendship and faithful mentorship, the past and future do matter. In these relationships, the past is gold, and the future is the promise of what might unfold from the creativity of our waking and sleeping dreams, at the very edge of words and in the collapse of boundaries that Jerry so long invited me into.

I invite you to find Jerry in *Defeat/No Surrender* and in his writings. These poems echo Jerry's studies and the writers and thinkers he swam with as he developed his own move toward We/Thee—I/Thou. Together they reflect my way of embodying Jerry's ideas and practices. He was a guardian of and a guide to the rich world to be discovered through imagination and hope.

Sonnet for Jerry

He offers a green card
He wears a green shirt
Sometimes with matching pants.
His smile is ear to ear
As the tree behind him is floor to ceiling
Like he is witnessing tikkun then and there.
In a fleeting moment his smile lifts sideways a little
When "of course"   "I'm here"
"I see the shadow you're afraid of"
Needs to be said. And it does.
You take the green card
You recognize the shadow is yourself
You know about wholeness now
And you know what love is.

Part I

Salvation, by all means

I Wish I Could Speak Yiddish Like Satchmo

My genie gave me 3 wishes and 3 more
If I use each third to ask for another set
Three times.

I wish I could sing and speak Yiddish like Satchmo.

I wish vanity were a green plastic colander
that drains out pride.

I wish I could talk to Simone Weil. So hard
To live close to your values.
I wish organic pet food made dogs piss
good for grass and flowers.

I wish farms and gardens could shove
evil back up the devil's asshole.

I wish cynicism was not my middle name,
my go-to.

I wish I could sing and speak Yiddish
like Satchmo. I really do.

The Devil Has No Secrets

I.   The devil has no secrets
      What you see is what you get.

      Simple yes and no
      Or else you go

      Off the rails
      Railing you didn't know,

      Like standing on your shoe lace
      While you try to tie it

      You can protest your innocence
      But you don't have a leg to stand on.

II.   The devil has no secrets,
      Django will tell you, his reeds
      With garlic and crucifix
                    syncopate
      The sounds of our future
                    history sans Satan—
      Une deux trois

There's a screech in the swallow and sway:
Giving out a warning,
                the devil is not new to jive
But clubfooted, he will trip.

III.   A whisper is not a secret.
        A bribe with or without rouge
                is not a gift.
        Soap under fingernails is enough to shift the scales—
        Chicken is not a game for Satan.
                still and all
        Chickens are the most populous birds,
                the best fed.
        They will go forth and multiply
        If we don't go extinct.

IV.   For some time genetic psychologists
        And oral historians have studied Mephistopheles
        Who, like superman, gets giddy
                under shiny Krypton debris.
        In a recent paper they wrote:
        We conclude out of an abundance of caution
                with a margin of error
                That the devil indeed has no secrets.

Genesis

"and it was good"
So followed seven days.
"It was good"
Each named so we know them
One after the other ....and make dates.
"and it was good"
A speck in time just ahead of names
(and numbers)
When pretty was not a map
to be filled in,
When friendly was not a rorshach
to be administered
(nor an emotional intelligence quotient).
"It was good"
Sun up and down
Moon shine...drunk
Before there's a name for sobriety.
"and it was good"
A speck in time just ahead of grammar
(and syntax)
When a kiss was just a kiss
(and a sigh was just that too)
When god had no name
And was still pondering what was good.

Abiding

Inspiration does not need assignable warrant
To have value
To abide.

Faith in care   given and expected
                       withheld and disappointed
Does not need figured worship

Idols are where zealot
                religion and science typos
Converge:
      good and evil QED
      ie: each is mercury looking
           for the other
Only: NO NO NO!
      why not let the absence of god
Be anonymous
The pain of not so good
The agony of being lost in cloud cover
      no separation between street and sidewalk

Inspiration does not require warrants
To be abiding.

Fly in Haman's Ointment

She can hear the whisper
                of waves
It's twilight in winter
When archangels sing
To confirm daylight will return

      who said to put the clock back
           that far?

To be precise:
This is no time to die.
Precision is the perennial poetry of fundamentals
After the dark season when the dock
Belongs to seagulls
Much as among immigrants (with boats at their backs
Encamped below 14th St.) the kitchen belonged
To the women
The way the beds in a harem
Belong to the wives
So even in the dark season Esther could move uptown

A French beret on her head
Felt…
                    an eyebrow squints a jaunt
The beret is pinned and still…
                    the pins pull her lips into smiling.

There is an Esther in the palace
                  a sveste
One who is everybody's skin and blister.
Uncle Mordechai is at the gate
He can foresee the colonels about to be hung.
While colonels and potiphars are selling jobs
To would-be executioners hungry for work.

(All around the canal gallows carpenters
Otherwise upholsterers, cabinet makers) men who build furniture
        as well as scaffolds
On Saturday some of them clean up well,
Covered up in white prayer shawls
                  and swaying.

For Esther, it was a time to dance.
Sumptuous and steaming
        virtue
        in its fullest bloom!
A fly in Haman's ointment.

The Impossible Is Possible

Put your hands to your ears
Keep out the noise
Steady your head.

If a rose could defy the breeze
It would.
That's why it can't imagine eternity.

No one wishes a flower long life when
A relative passes. Yet a gardener
Nurses for longevity.

Because if the impossible is possible
What is impossible?

Existential is the color of light
      in an unlit garden
Always just a little east of Eden
Becoming.

Intoxication

Chastity
      without covet
      without apathy
Else virtue is dull
Vice is denigrating
Diminishing brain food
To fanatics
      marooned on low tide
      indulgence
Without innocence:

Gratitude hanging from a tree
      crow fruit
      cryo cherry
In stagnant martinis
      unfreezing
      melting with creosoted ice
Burning up from the inner belly
      stuffed in frenzy
With dull
      and denigrating
           excess.

Improv
(After Philo)

Jazz
      take some skin…
So it begins
      always with skin
As do we
      life is in the skin
      thick and thin
Attended and unattended

Keep your own record
      akashic legacy

Improv   bricolage
      the meaning
      in the relation we are
In the frost melting
Floundering in self regard   in the style
      of prophets:
      the 44,000 year old cave Chagall
      the bugler Bird Parker
      low hanging fist
The ambition chisel blunts after anonymous use
You can see the busker

Say goodbye in English:
        so many rules
But with jazz accompaniment
        so many exceptions,

Bringing love to truth

Just as when that white bird
        flies by again
        winking
In the rain   it's that old
        that predestined.

You must know
        how joy inflates like a barrage balloon
        how trust invites hope
        the way laughter takes carbon out of the air
        how to put one foot in front of the other
        and not step in shit.

Salvation, by all means

Don't   dignify dismal
Squeeze your nose inhale

Dismal is the rotting eggs
That won't digest

Or road kill
Days later.

Put it in a sack of mud
Add bricks

Throw it with the strength of Samson
Bring down the house, into the nearest water.

See yourself smiling
Yarzeit for your buried grief.

Be a cataclysm of joy
For the you rendezvous in the house of the lord

With love in the abductive
At last.

Salvation,
by all means.

Moved by a Mountain

He was not a small man
      not tall
Sitting at the foot of a medium sized
Mountain
      his arm embracing the ground
      wearing a rustic hat
      rakishly.

He proposed his love for the mountain
He proposed marriage
He promised the mountain
To keep its surname
      Etna.

No need to get hot and bothered
He could take no for an answer
      such was his love.

The mountain was moved
      because of his love for it.

Self Improvement

A boy reads a book
        to improve himself
He looks in a mirror where an angel
Looks at him
        neither knows what to say.

The same boy returns to his book
        to improve himself further
Until he has to pee
        to relieve himself,
That feels better.

Better is a good feeling
        good is better
        he tries tries tries hard
Still he can't find good reading
        to himself   even out loud.

His uncle said the book would get him there
His father argued for Guinness:
        "Drink and grow, you'll see!"

Honor your father can be heard from the mirror:
        drink the Guinness!

The same boy reads heavier books now
        he can carry two or three
                at once.

He looks in the mirror
        they have both gained some weight.

Today, Tomorrow.

I get wrapped up watching ducks
Bobbing between rocks brushing by barnacles
No memory of the pain.
A feather is a feather is a feather
It bounces back
Akin to women bearing children
No matter the pain soon forgotten.
Pain is not meant to last.

And so, questions follow:
       can you bob?
       can you lighten as a feather?
       can you bounce back
Today?
Tomorrow?

Scarecrow Me

I bring in my
Scarecrow self.
My head is left behind
My pants are waisted
For another
My hands
      like my eyes
Wrinkle
      regretfully
As if the sun went down afraid.
I frighten
      myself
      away
The crows hover.
They see the truth.
They flap
      when I blink.
In between
I have the chance
Of my life.

Sabbath

The dream of sabbath rest
Has Jung's archetype of liberation in it
Freud's complex of desire
Joyce's immodest tumescence
The Lord's Prayer high on vintage wine
Zohar mirrors, backed by ice not mercury
To cool the howl of poets
Struggling to free a mind trapped in rules
Like a rabbit in an OCD forest
Longing in a garden of indigo and myrrh
In a weekly rebirth of wonder.

Freud

It's not about being wrong
It's about believing
The thought you form
Is a master stroke.
Not just a sacrifice of mind
On the alter
Of human longing.

It's not about being right
It's about
           discerning
The acne in the most beautiful
Representations of human logic.

Why else
Would those who seek to be healed
Be called on to be patient?
And those called to heal
Be perpetually practicing?

Me Real/You Real

Come out of the shadow
You unknown friend
Come out
Let me see you
Let me present my broken bow
My blunted arrow
My bitten finger nails
My right hand reaching
To release the blind
Obscuring the light
That exposes
Me to you.

Holiness

G cell
Thorny neurons
In the crown
Where conscience
Counsels will.

Tinctures
For growing holly
With smooth edges…

Oh that's the G in god
The communion gene,
Once the immune system
Could maybe benefit from
Supplements.

Oh but
But oh
What if that's why
We have an alphabet
Oh but
But oh
Why
We have an alphabet.

False Witness

People will talk: a

Rust red killim   for a coat. In the snow

It's 40% holes
Not the ones that sell for 20k dollars.

People will talk: he

Must have stolen   it
Cats pissed all over
               it

Nobody should wear
A frayed and soaked killim rug   for
                  a
Coat   in the snow

Without people talking.

People will talk   see
Matted eyebrows   wisp bald
His eyes down the field empty
Like Lear in the dark.

The windows   on his soul
                 in the snow
                 bleeding
On the rug   he must have stolen

Crows eager   to feast.

People talk.

(Heidegger's) They

Facing the Dictatorship of
    (Heidegger's) They

In 1908
NYC forbade women
From smoking in public
        She had he did, and
Oral sex died

dead to the degenerated public
macula

Until the City forbade everybody
From smoking in public
        She had he had, and
The internet blasted privacy
Out of the muniment room

dead to the degenerated public
macula

Tearing wiped by yellow-stained fingers
In the 'fruitful and multiply' salute

Humility who's he?
                she?
                they?
Whose chosen pronoun?
Better an adverb:
                maybe.

Who Can Stop Them

If the people don't want/to come to the ball field/Who can stop them/.

The birds are high/On pot/In the park/No longer on helium/Leaking/out of birthday balloons.

Even above/the furnace smoke/
The errant finch inhales/intoxicating fumes/The bare breast robin almost collides/With a murder of plastic bags/Floating above the tree line/.

Outliers want something stronger/
They pray to give it form/They fly
In circles criss cross diameters/To reverse their logic/

They sing/in oppositions/
Flap their wings/in anticipation/
Pierce the core/of what they know/
A chorus signals direction/

Outliers all....

If the rest don't want/To come/who/
Can anyone stop them/.

Moses Rose Up

Moses rose
When he struck the rock
Moses rose up
When he struck the rock

Moses rose up
       in shock
What a shock! What a shock!
When he hit that rock

Out came the water
And the ground he stood on shook
He could feel the ground
       oh how it shook

When Moses struck the rock
       with his stick

Moses hit the rock with his stick
And it split
Out poured the water
When he split the rock

Moses cried with the water
And all the people cried.

Tarot

It is widely believed
           the Tarot
And the 52-card pack
Were designed as code
To protect wisdom
From Inquisitors.

It is believed
The Tarot
           and the 52-card pack
(as is the weeks of the year)
Embody wisdom
Separated from avid watchers
Themselves under the surveillance
           of Inquisitors.

It is believed the Tarot
(22 Arcanum as in the letters of the Hebrew alphabet)
And the 52-card pack
           (with two Jokers)
Are wisdom laughing out loud.

Release

Thinking itself is/ a form of exit/ like god/
Catching Adam looking/ like himself/ thinking/
The 1,2,3 million year old/ bashed in skulls/
By whoever/ thinking/ like god/ catching someone/
Or other/ looking like himself/ thinking.

Tectonic/ fighting and biting/ scaffolded/ nuclear
Canon and bows/ biting nails/ sucking out green lights/
Retching up red/ like god/ stop/ in the headlights/ stop/
Thinking/ stop.

A little light/ in all of us/ god thinking/
In us as in trees/ in the tides/ god/ reason/ we are/
God's children/ grown up/ with trees/ gods?/ bands
Of angels?

Music/ thinking larynx/ scrubbing tongue/ tides/ sucking
Out the green/ go/ leave/ retching up red/ grown up/
Gods/ stop/ in the music/ stop/ thinking/ stop.

Listen to/ to the angels singing/ on the snake river/
Devilish riptide wind/ tide/ raft faster/ horses/ white water/
Angels shouting/ singing loud in forest/ devilish chorus/ thinking/
Betting on even/ red/ blood green/ thinking/

Thinking/ thinking/ gods row/ stop/ betting on even/ stop/
Stop.

Or/ capsize/ heavy heads/ not good swimmers/ angel dust inflates
Stars/ like god/ perform thinking/ shooting constellations/
Biting/ down till cuticles bleed/ seeing red/
Thinking green/ stop/ thinking/ like god
Performs thinking.

Like/ looking for like/ angel dust inflates/ wings/
Stars/ shocking/ biting/ uniforms and teams/ murders of
Crows/ singing/ dancing benevolent/ out of character/
Like angels/ to sweeten your tea/ and toast/ enjoy/
Biting toast and nails/ forgot/ nails grow back/ an angel
Sucks her thumb/ sore thumb thinking/ like god/ holding his
Breath/ not to stop/ to want/ to want/ to inhale/
Angel dust inflates/ stork on the wing/ on the/
Snake river/ white water/ sucking up green/ stop/
Stop on red/ stop/ stop/ perform thinking/ like god?/
Hear the ozone squeak/Like angels?

Not one angel/wants to fight/Release/.

Freud removes Spinoza's/Picture from his wall/
Turn the corner/it's down/to the gene/
like it/or not/the gene/god thinking
         Is why/you've got/what you've got/

    what else to pray for/
        but release.

Foil

11 windows. 22 top and bottom
Aluminum foil strips on each one
Waving like nervous ribbons
Chased by a vacuum cleaner signifying a warning
To birds: GLASS.

I have broken my nose running into a glass door.
I have heard birds splat splay splat. We have seen
Crashing and dying here. The first cause
Of the funicular foil:
                splat oh dear
                splat oh well

Moving on. Not St. Francis clone
She does not shrug off any death.
Consider she says: if beauty is in the eye of the beholder
                every creature with eyes must be saved.

As Time Passes

I. As time passes new time came and went, as time passes old time goes underground, as time passes born again perennials come and go, as time passes hydrangea headed boffins bloom, invent, as time passes their scribes compose propositions, as time passes prophecy gauntlets with destiny for justification, as time passes judgement and confident agree
to give away their daughter to a salesman, as time passes the bet pays off and doesn't, as time passes alters give way to alters, as time passes eternity beckons, as time passes those who are succulent and righteous kneel on rocks and bleed, as time passes eternity solves unsolved equations, and as time passes the bloody beg for miraculous staunching "let this be blood enough" they cry as time passes.

II. The willow came back a second time. This time I agreed. I had never shaved a tree. I have shaved young men before their beards to practice, them and me, when I was in barber school. The willow was a first. All was well until I nicked it. Not like I could apply a hard stick of cream to stop bleeding as I do with men. The sap would not stop. There was so much weeping.

I ruined a dozen towels trying to staunch the sap.
The willow bore me no grudge. When
I see the tree on the street it always waves a leaf.

Essential

What is essential
To whom?
Whom to who?
Forget grammar
What's essential is the point.
If grammar is essential
Like nurses like sanitation hombres
Like ingrained dirt
Like inherent compassion
Don't forget
Indignity is done to.
Done to is not essential.
Except not everybody agrees.
It is essential to some
For others to suffer indignity.

The Essenes according to Flavius Josephus
Were kinder than other sects.
Without Rome and coliseum bloodletting
Kindness might have been   might have been
Essential   to more!
The row boat will be oared
The dart will have a board.
What's a shooting range without a target

What kind of shooter misses it?
It's in the essence of function.

Function like horseness is not a live animal
Before there is a rider in the saddle
Charging through a village picking up people
Like chattel, or before a hero rides in
With food for the hungry, rides in to rescue
A sweetheart fall in love with her family
Pray for the children of another sister
The one who does not look like family.
Is there a general stigmatic in creation
Like horseness?
Did horses in the beginning stigmatize
Horses with finger and toes
So easily crushed by those with hooves
Like lepers
Like shades of skin marking off
Those to be crushed?
How essential were hooves to horseness
Or fingers and toes to horseness?

Did they leave bitter fruits at the bottom of the hill
Where lust and consequence lie.
Of course consequence is essential
As are polar shifts which we are told
With certainty is all about blame
The original sour fruit.
Like boys killed by police on Weds and Fridays

Like anybody killing anybody on Suns and Thursdays
So many geometric shapes:
Kneel and choke
On what planet   Who would have thought …

You know angels.
They don't have to be invisible.
Those are wings on her cleaning the bedpan
Those are wings on him hauling off garbage
Surely those must be wings swaddling your babies
And Prime is all wings and the will to fly
Across borders, over oceans, to bring the angelness
In creation to your stoop.
There are wings on those who guard prisoners,
On those exonerated, those justly imprisoned
Instead of us. It is time it is time
To grow a pair and see who since the beginning
Has carried the potential to be seen.
Repeat for 6 days and pray for rest.

A Chimp in the Mirror

If there were nothing fallen
          autumn might look
          like spring.

Erectus is a comic state
            makes some men cry
To see a chimp in the mirror
Others laugh and chase their tails.

There is a teaching
"Every fear is everybody's fear"
It's corollary
"Every dream is everybody's dream"
          why not
Why shouldn't your bloody feet
          ache in my boots?

A lone chimp hides the twist
          in his weave
Longing to unwind
          sensing death
Could be a corrosion of imagination.

Meditation

Roll out the yoga mat
The purple one is good
Promotes an imperial reach in some.

But like a used magic carpet
This mat has hobbled horse power
And you are bone tired.

Look out at the pond, fish popping
Gulls predating the loping basil leaf
The ballerina in the bend of the tree

Opens her left thigh. She lets go.
Attachment is suffering ripeness is not nothing
Roll up the mat
The presence of absence.

Such a Shame

Such a shame
To have missed the chance
Like Lawrence with his snake at Etna.

Such a shame
To never get the chance
To see only your bruised yellow toenail.

Such a shame
To have stepped on another's toes
To bleeding.

Such a shame
To be stepped on
As an easy mark.

Such a shame to feel your face
Features and shape
In belief they began with you.

Who can't remember
The color of the pants you wear
Without looking down.

Such a shame to lean hard on your pen
As if a prosthetic
While the author's desk eats the author—

Or the splinters in the author's mouth
Settle in…
It's not a new idea of human.

It's the same old coming and going:
Here comes the night
Here comes the day.

Such a shame
To miss the point.

Contrition

The blindfold can come off
Faust told Mephistopheles.
The NDA was cancelled
He took a kneel.
Like St. Paul he found out
The blindfold can come off.
It was a long distance run
Just had to read the Lord's Prayer
Then go rescue Dorian Gray
And ask if he knew why the Earth
                      does not trust us.
Because he is said to say, because
                      we are afraid to kneel.
That's why the blindfold can come off
                      kneeling,
Can be like hammer and nail in a corner
                      hard to reach.
Doesn't have to be wear a black cap
                      not a death sentence.
Contrition works. The blindfold
                      can come off.

Imagining Heschel
"Racism: maximum of hatred for a minimum of reason"

HESCHEL

(In his morning class at the Jewish Theological Seminary)

Good morning.
I was almost late to class this morning. When I went to the elevator, a neighbor, I think her name is Louise, wanted to tell me about how grateful she is for the new radiators in our building.

I am sorry to those I have kept waiting.

We have spoken before of Father Bertrand. Remember he is the Christian missionary from whose book I read to you. (*He recites*) "They said to me don't go to the shanties, you will find only whores and sun baked poverty. I went anyway, and ten years later I reported back, poverty persists, hard as clay, but I have not yet met a whore."

There is no "other," my friends. The "other" is a fragment of our fears. So we will read this man's experience and discuss it from a Jewish perspective.

Yes. . . yes, I know - this is the reflection of a Christian Brother, serving in a Christian Mission.

Let me tell you about my neighbor in the elevator Louise.

Salvation, by all means | 57

So each morning I go down in the elevator and sometimes we stop at the third floor. Louise gets on and she says to me: "Good morning Alan." Now, as you well know, my name is not Alan. This started about four years ago. But anyway, she says, "Good morning Alan." By now, I actually look forward to her and to my being called Alan. Why?

Because I feel a certain freedom when she calls me Alan. For a few seconds I am free of the identity I carry with me as Abraham. I do not feel mistaken or misidentified. Rather, I am reminded of how I might be different from whom I have become. I am reminded that who I am is open to discovery as well as to recognition.

So Jewish seminarians — you can put themselves into the shoes of Christians for a moment. Perhaps you will find the freedom to open yourselves, to find a little bit more of yourselves than you are used to.

Part II

Defeat/No Surrender

Auntie, What's the Resistance?
(After a reminiscence of Tina Anselmi)

Her beret
Olive with a dark red cocktail cherry
Gave Eden its jaunty look
Grass its green.
She bore children in its coziness
Carried fruit and vegetables
To cook il pranzo la cena.

Her olive beret
Brought water from the lake
Made a nest for playing house
With dolls. At times knives
Hidden in it carried under arm.
In epochal moments molotov gunpowder
In the folded felt…the cocktail cherry
Was a giveaway. But too late.

She dampened the cloth to wipe the froth
Of anguish, dry it in the sun
To bring remains home.
She had spare as needed
To carry fruit and vegetables
To cook il pranzo la cena,
To kiss both cheeks and sing:
Buon appetito... buon appetito.

Swords into Plowshares

At the end of WW1 soldiers returned esophagus
                                      shot through with gas.
Flu landed battalions in a second front
                                      blunting
Leftover dreams. Wives cut vet's moody hair
                                      bip bop bip bop on a kitchen chair.
Every strand knotting a held back a scream
                                      rage rage at his shattered spleen.
After rubbing her ring for years like Aladdin's lamp
                                      she massages the cramp
Out of her fingers. He winces at himself in the mirror
                                      he feared death would be his barber
Not the scissor: "swords into plowshares in this spot?
                                      Bip bop bip bop why not."

Just a Thought

Depth charge/change and a solitary thought
Aimed at the man who won't recognize his dance step
Is a thought, his sit down to sip cognac is a thought,
His trip on parquet floor to the toilet another, his tip
To the waiting for it waiter yet another.
My aim will change that and I will be charged.
See me in the stocks, or on my hind legs
Like the backside of a human horse act.
I am kicking at the door of a party for a man
Who won't recognize thinking. The barn door
Hits me in the arse, I feel my fingers melting
Like birthday candles after happy birthday is sung.
Wincing at wax on my fingers is a thought, charging
Out for ice cold water in the trough on the street
Is another. Taking stock/aim yet another.

Love in Quarantine

"I'll have to rearrange myself"
She says as I put my head on her lap
Which makes me cry like I never have.
Geese take the check in my palms
As an exit cue. The family waddles to the water
In a hurry like the Van Trapps escaping Salzburg.
When the father hits the pond he rests his head
On the mother's shoulder. She flutters
Which makes him cry, which makes her cry,
Which makes the children feel comforted.

One Eye of Jesus

Chaos in chorus
Turmoil in e pluribus

Singing good lord save us
Good lord save us!

Everything is rhesus
Through one eye of Jesus

Looking through just one eye
        one eye
        of Jesus

                cry Hosanna
                Zanna Zanna

The other eye weeps
Blood freezes rain

Again and again
Looking through just one eye of Jesus

Blood freezes rain
        the morning sun wanes

> *cry Hosanna*
> *Zanna Zanna*

Looking through the one eye
> just one eye
> of Jesus

> *cry Hosanna*
> *Zanna Zanna*

Sound out the chorus
Cry out for forgiveness

Looking through the third eye
> the third eye
> of Jesus

> *cry Hosanna*
> *Zanna Zanna*

It all looks like rhesus
Through one eye of Jesus
Sound loud the chorus
Cry out for forgiveness
Looking through the third eye
> the third eye
> of Jesus.

Emma Lazarus

Emma Emma Emma Lazarus
Wake yourself up   wake yourself up
         like Lazarus

You've played dead
         too long
You've played dead
         way too long
         too long.

Fire burns in water
And the little child shall swim in it.
Her heart fills with fear
While mountains move to nourish her.

Emma Emma Emma Lazarus
I know you're made of stone
But you see the children come
         get sent home
Emma Emma Lazarus
         you gotta moan.

Fire burns the water
And the little child shall boil in it.
All the flowers feel the tears in him
The lilies come to soothe his skin.

Emma Emma Lazarus
      a woman seen what you've seen
      gotta have a moan in her
Surely Emma Lazarus
A woman like you Emma
      Emma Emma Lazarus
      got to rise up
Like Lazarus
      gotta find your moan.

Fishers of Men

When they were called
                to be fishers of men
                they sold their boats
Bought piccolos
The sound could be heard in the seventh skin
                of the inner ear.

A hurricane blew up
The light bulbs blew out
The ghosts trembled
(a hurricane is not good for ghosts).
You can hear them sing entirely off key.
Beer in their spittle on their tongues
                on their kisses.

Their lips are made of leather.
Like a cat of nine tails
                they sting.

Let us pray the fishermen say.
One takes out a razor from a smart phone
He sits on a prayer mat   takes out a razor
                shaves the rug.

He feels absurd
Absurd is the sound of his razor now.

Heard in the seventh skin
                    of the inner ear.

and the choir sings
(After reading Pascal Quignard)

I.   Is it barbaric
    To use expired chemicals
    For lethal injection
    Just to say *go to hell?*

    Is it barbaric
    To freeze water to keep it
    From those who can't pay
                  the owners of water?
                    the owners
                          of water!

    Does it all come down from Barabas?
                    what he did?
                          what they did for him?

    The preacher reads: the tears we dry
                          are old.
    The choir sings: *humm*
                    humm

II. In the country
Silos stand like steeples to welcome
Fretful congregations.
Woods sway in a light wind
As minyans moving toward each other.
In both directions
        the other is there.

A global epidemic of ill will
A zeitgeist full of it.
Widespread viral contagion—
        congregants can't sing
        minyans are down to one.

The preacher reads: the tears we dry
                are old.
The choir sings: *humm*
            humm

III. The echo of a dream deferred
Is in the sun rising and setting
        setting
            rising
The muzak of longing
And the pseudo sanctity of choosing.
The boundary of the land of not forgetting.
Listening for an Ur sound.

The preacher reads: the tears we dry
                                        re old.

The choir sings: *humm*
                            humm

The Ascent of Man

Rebel engineers rehung crucifixion
By adding metal joints to the horizontals,
So they stretch sideways.
By adding a spring to the metal joints
The horizontals gain a vertical range.

When a new born boy pees
In his father's face
A week after circumcision
You know both testaments make sense:
        the end of child sacrifice
        and
        baptism

        vibrations in the eye of the watcher

The site of the beginning held open
        with matchsticks

Not to prevent winking
Not to abandon sleep

Vibrations in the devil's promise
    thou shalt not die

The first double entendre

No death
But death

Did an ape ever crucify an ape?
What's next?

Hitchcock Through the Eyes of a Bird

He is always in view
In one take or another
Easy to miss:
(Big brother watching, good samaritan
Stopping, selfish passing by, shy lover
Waiting, embodied spirit anticipating
Being recognized.)
His flourine eyes give him depth.
Not deep as in the sight of birds
But with range enough to see himself.

"Look at me!" "Look at me!" Mistake to translate
Across species. He believed his fears of girls,
(Whom he called birds in his youth) was everybody's shame.

That terrible avian rage he filmed was my
Extended family wrapped in fury we've never understood.
Lost in the hollow of beseeching wings
Held up to the fingerling light burning on
Phlegmatic phone lines.

We've been here so long, much longer.
Hitchcock's finger to his nose, knew.

Lady Macbeth Tells it Like it is

When she broke her   foot
She thought yes now I can play the piano
               for myself

A child finds herself through mirroring
(Birds listen to their parent's song before singing)

When her mother used the moon to excuse herself
It was a no brainer: who likes a lazy woman?
Not her father.

Giving the sun the winter off
Who likes that?

Both pessimism and optimism
Sounding like an out of tune church organ
Piss her off.

Don't sing me a love song, she insists.
Her needles click like drum sticks.
Knitting is a string process
Along the slow wobble
       of the earth's circumference.

Her husband spends hours disentangling
        shirt hangers
Trying to save one throw out others

Breaks the pitcher on his nightstand
        in the twist
There are always pieces to pick up
        or not pick up

Maybe the wind sings a different tune
        in different places?

What if I could take a self
Out of mothballs
She wonders, he wonders too:

I have become the idol of myself
I am without a self,
Canned meat: my voice has only
Antique music in it.

I notice how often I bang my elbows
Against door frames cabinets glass shower walls

Boundaries were never a problem
Boundaries are a cosmic spasm

Props in a theatre of war
A surgical precision.

All the world is a stage.

2 Cheers for the 1 Eyed Citizen

    2 cheers for the 1 eyed citizen
    Squinting in the light of a paraffin lantern

I loved a dream which brained me.
Took out my right eye.
My dream was arranged in words.
Recitation impaled me against a wall
Where it was curfew 24/7.
Sun and moon are tied tight in ropes
My dream called herself Law.
She took off her clothes, submerged.
She shook a sword. Called me:
You think you can make the waves succumb?
Spots broke out all over my body
Which she counted.
What she counts she owns.
People around me in uniform all wearing my skin.

    2 cheers for the 1 eyed citizen

She took a bath,
Her tricolor wrapped around her blade
Nicking herself shaving her legs.

No excuses. The faithful
Turned a blind eye.

The storm was always coming
Everybody who feels could feel it.
No one knew it
Friends mothers fathers children mothers
No one talked about the storm
They couldn't
They didn't know it
They only felt it.

        2 cheers for the 1 eyed citizen

Birdsong and leafy tenors
In their branches.
There are those who beg the rain to stop
Others pray
For the drought to end.
People cheer her on.
    she scrinches
    her tattoo stings.
All in limbo
TV ads fill her mind.
Her heart is poured into five pound sacks
Of sugar, which she sells
Day after day.

2 cheers for the 1 eyed citizen
Always faithful.
CLAP CLAP
More cheers   hip hip
            (canned laughter)

Patriot

I. General faces his troops to cheer them knowing his medals
underneath the fur are cutting his skin he doesn't mind
the wet drip of bleeding no deeper than expected yes!
expected by a man with four stars to comfort him on clear
and overcast nights ready to give gifts of his memorabilia
from his heart, Purcell in his mind is metal and hail melting
softening his lenses further than his last prescription for
today he dreams of all those he has swaddled in the flag
not thinking about birth, only resurrection.

II. Nothing happening with the plough and sword
The powder dust is itchy
Tangled in the soldier's nose hair

                the weave
                the screen
                barbed wire on the drone

Picturing soldiers still able to crawl
Not like a baby born to crawl
To stand.
The crawling soldiers may never stand.

                      the beginning is over.
           wither the mise-en-scène?

the baby

              the soldier

   the weave

             the web

beginning over.

The Sweet Shop Poem

How sweet is sugar
When it's born?
Before it's a candy.
Before it's a thirst for chocolate.
The rotting function takes time
Pleasure before filling and extraction.

My mother was friends with a crippled man
Who came to the shop to buy cigarettes
And a chocolate bar. She didn't charge
For the chocs. She never said why.
I think she understood the continuum.

My father made the day after Monday
Before Wednesday a thunderous celebration:
Sugar was liberated from post war rationing
FOR CHILDREN ONLY…all day no adults,
The shop was a child's playroom, Smarties
Were everyone's favorite. I loved the colors.

A Jamaican doc bought Suchard Swiss chocs
Each week and Smarties for his kids.
Mum sent suffering children his way:
Kids burned by firecrackers, scrapped in fighting,
Cut on broken beer bottles, dislocated fingers
And shoulders off a skidding bike, sick on sun bleached
Candy mushrooms.

His, the long view: He gave each one a lollipop.

Neighbors

On this country road
Neighbors used to wave say hello
None unwelcome.
Now the magnet that brings hands to touch
      Is in for repair.
Where's the evidence of friendship
When all the ways into that great castle
      are guarded
           guarded with gallons of detergent
      and spray?
Enough to make a tree branch weep
           to make a bird's throat sore.

What Is a Revolution

Pundits say *"god bless America"*
Panhandlers tell you *"god bless you"*
(Whether you give or not)

This is a chaplaincy of the street:
        "Our prayers are with you.
        We mourn for your loss."
Deep in the heart of hearts
Who gives a toss?

It would take a revolution.

What is a revolution?
It's always on the street.
She tells me.
I can feel her palm cup my face.
Isn't it grand how the palm fits the face.

St. Augie

Augie's voice crossed from fisherman to fisherman
Baritones and tenors from boat to boat. From tank
To tank. Call and response alternatively deployed.
Before and after. After after.
Augie went mad.
His medical chart confirms he still is.
Calls himself St. Augustine.
His Confessions his life's work.

He claims (confesses) he is guilty of everything:
For after and after after.
When he was no saint.

The priest at the hospital, father Raphael,
Gave Augie a bible. Both testaments like chariot horses
For to carry a wounded soldier. The nurse's aid, Rita,
Reported he liked to catch flies with the book: opened it,
Honed in like a sniper, snapped it dead between pages.
He always confessed.

St. Augie confessed: he voted wrong. He lied
About his ballistics know how. He had never given
Up smoking. He confessed he forgot god once.
His tank only had room for two. It was his fault
What happened to separate skin from bone.
He confessed he knew his infection caused Dr. Nye
To go mad in the field base surgery. He confessed
When he killed flies he was reminded of battle. They like he
Had nothing left to lose. Like a wet dream, with the blood
Wrung out of it.

He confessed he lied about quitting smoking.
He never gave blood. He had been afraid of school
And dreamed of showing up naked. He was afraid of battle.
He dreamed of showing up naked. He confessed he once
Blamed god and his children for making him miss them.
It was he who by dark raised up half mast flags. He was not ready
To be dead. Why, the priest asked, did he rip his nurse's crucifix
From her throat? He was confused, he confessed, by the color
Of her skin.

Ought Not Be But It Is

Kneeling should tell the tale
Of a simple act of contrition
Of courage
Of awe and humility
But it's not.

Kneeling might be a signal
For readiness to serve
Of devotion
Of awe and humility
But it isn't.

Kneeling could be hammer on nail
Of craft in difficult corners
Of repair
Of awe and humility
But it's not.

Kneeling ought not be a gun position
For death sentencing
Of suffocating sweaty sadism.
But it is.

Unsettled Minds

Jersey lights hang like suspended fall leaves.
In Manhattan the sun is burning off roof-top frost.
It's day and night across the Hudson.

Hoists are rising, roofs are wet
as if irate devines have been spitting
all night on Manhattan. There's a dry rustle
of pedestrian and bike traffic
along still rank tar sidewalks.

Bridges, tunnels, and ferries are strikingly quiet.
An avalanche of lament comes from choral mists
jostling the heavy air over Staten Island. The smell
of coffee from Hoboken is stale, Sinatra's digitized voice
sounds empty like an echo in an abandoned church.

Draft riot debris flies back and forth,
criss-crossing the Verazzano.
Hair follicles suck up the lead in the air
unsettling commuter minds.

Dixit

Hieroglyphs
        ideas   impressions.
Someone coughs: ahem ahem
        words
          "the thing is the thing is the thing."

The Rosetta Stone was cleaned off
        in three languages.
        Just one
would have left it indecipherable.

Someone else coughs: ahem ahem
         "How does it feel to say that?"
        Freud dixit.

Interior canaries and muskrats
         run about frantically.

Sapiens the tamer uses words.
The circus is only maximus
if no one coughs: ahem ahem.
        Sandberg dixit:
         "Where do we go from here?"

Oh My

The way it's said urine sterilizes a wound
or the way blood transfused is supposed to reclaim the soul,
the way truth frays
when dragged from the earth like coal,
the way coal can it's said burn clean—
but look at a miner's face,
just look at a miner's face,
there's the truth.

Oh my, the grass is not greener
anywhere. Ubiquitous cameras
convict the dogs who pine to piss on your gardens.
Oh gardeners   Oh gardeners
put down your bags, pick up your guns,
you are soldiers now.
Oh soldiers   Oh soldiers
Why not sing songs of hope and glory?
And blink a little of "there but for the grace—"

Hand of the Sun

You know how a pot rattles
when water runs thin and sprout steam exudes
a warm flatulence.

You know how you want something to happen
so much there's no wonder left
thick enough to fill a pocket,
just expectations stitched up in the lining.

You know how you grieve for what's gone wrong,
anorexic listing toward skin and bone,
even though the hand of the sun is on your back.

Up and Down

Going up
out of suffering.
Elevator coming down
picking up ingredients
                  spoiled
                  freshly picked
from gardens that are more magical than we know
                  or less
                  much less—
but what's more,
                  yes, what's more?

Defeat/No Surrender

Research ornithologists say they can prove
All birds, robins plovers osprey doves
See colors we cannot see or fashion
Permutations of color we cannot imagine.

There are five smoke alarms in my apartment
One is deceitful:
>> It's quiet when I light a candle
>> It screams when the AC is on.

Victors usually don't remember
The signs of resistance in the body
> That proclaim no surrender.

Yes! No surrender
>> It's in the   twist of the shoulder in the morning.
>>   in the smile of the leaf on the skylight.

Children's games   ropes and ladders
Or the one where each player tries

To beat the crow hungry for cherries.
Like any adult day.
The devil bites his tail
                bleeding
                through the bandage,

The cock always crows thrice.

Obedience is a grudging devotion

But what are children of lesser gods to say
                                  to do

When the pergola of our house
Is grown full of wisteria?

A heron has been visiting for days.
We've seen eye to eye at times.
She has the movement in stillness   of a dancer
She scoffs at admiration
She tells me humans are quite
Adorable shades of color.

If I were a freshwater pond
I would tighten my flow
I would cry into my shorelines
If I were a Tuscan peasant bread
Or an Irish soda loaf I would be gluten free.
If a bayonet were a steak knife
I would eat with my fingers.

If torpedoes were genitals
I would have to be celibate.

You know?
No
Really?
Look...

I don't want to argue
                anymore
About war   about the system.
I want to laugh out loud
                at the words
Arranged like buttons and button holes
                to cover
Naked power.

I don't want to kill termites
                anymore
Because I can and I hate them.
They live for 24 hours
So I never know if I'm killing
                the young or old
And if I did
                who might I spare
Or not.

No I don't want to argue

Anymore
About Defeat or Surrender
About the morality of pulling weeds.
I want to kiss everybody's lips
          dry and blistered
Instead of making arguments
          about the young
And the old and who might be spared
          or not.

Imagine that!

When God Had No Name

I stopped rowing
Sat and stared
At a sparsely budding stalk
1 1/2 ft thin
And still (as far as I could tell)
Growth in it
But no intention.

I became fixed on the nature
Of no intention..
And of poets (I don't know why)
Who write about death
Intending to commune or rail.

The stick stands stark still
(no intention to stand its ground).
I could cut it, whittle it to make toys
Or leave it alone...

I was reminded again of poets
(I don't know why)
Who write about death:
Dreary days, flowers cut in mid-bloom,
Balloons losing air.

I saved a stink bug that day
Pulling him off the gauze kitchen curtain
After a jury of joists and jurists of roof tile
Condemned and sentenced him.
A pneumatic drill pounds hard…
Isn't it time to ask for whom and why
           we die
Like old batteries run dry
Pushing wagon loads of words
           about words.

I don't have a left position on all this.
I do have Munch's screaming face in mind.

Meanwhile you have to wonder how the silt phlegm
Of greed puts the brain to sleep,
Infects the bloodstream with splinters
Of dog collar righteous less ness
So that the room, you might recall it,
Where compassion is stored is cordoned off,
The garden where fidelity is grown
Is overrun by goose shit. The country
Where joy once fanned the sun
Like a soft palm is boarded up.
Prison cells are five star studio flats
For politicians and the bros
Who hire them, flabby in the creases
Yet robed in ermine.
A speck in time just ahead of names (and numbers)

A speck in time just ahead of grammar (and syntax)
When a kiss was just a kiss
(and a sigh was just that too)
When god had no name
And was still pondering what was good.

Thou Shalt Not Stand Idly By

It's a trip
How well-meaning can take you
Through forests of need,
Broken twigs begging for repair,
Flower petals crying out for help.
A well-meaning person can trip over needs
In the weeds. Trip into an auto-righteous zone,
Trip into walls of uncaring glue
And leaking pollen.

Thou shalt not, but how not?

A few notes from an improvised minyan
Like a jazz sextet coupled with a chamber quartet
Bear witness to any and all behavior:
The gun that goes off accidentally,
Shaming until stones are dressed in skin
Then lost in grinds of denial.

How not?

Find a sanctuary in a sabbath of your making.
Tell Ishmael and Ham hello.
Tell each we know all about cracked twigs,
Our petals like theirs can blossom from the smell of decay.
Bring mercy home to your parent's hearth
And be faithful to her.

About the Author

Colin Greer is president of the New World Foundation which supports activism and advocacy on behalf of the environment, democracy, and community-power building. Formerly a CUNY professor, Greer is a founding editor of *Social Policy Magazine* and a former contributing editor at *Parade Magazine*. He has authored and edited several books on education, ethnicity, immigration, and ethics. A poet and playwright, He has published two books of poetry, *Gnashing My Teeth* and *If But My Gaze Could Heal*. His plays have appeared in off-broadway productions, some of which can be found in his book, *Religious Differences Between Artichokes*. Never a moment to spare, Greer also serves on several not-for-profit boards, including the American Institute for Mental Imagery (AIMI).

About Dr. Jerry Epstein

Dr. Jerry Epstein (1935 – 2019) was a psychotherapist, healer, and spiritual teacher. Trained as a psychiatrist in the 1960s, he found psychiatry lacked answers to the major existential, ethical, and moral questions at the heart of his patients' ailments. Seeking the keys to physical, psychological, and spiritual healing, he apprenticed for nine years under the spiritual master, Colette Aboulker-Muscat, learning the "Kabbalah of Light," a 4,000 year-old western spiritual tradition. Jerry pioneered a groundbreaking, phenomenologically-based therapy that used transformative imagery (visualization) to heal emotional and physical issues. A prolific author, Jerry's wisdom lives on through his books, and his school, the American Institute for Mental Imagery (AIMI).

AIMI, a school for integrative health and spirituality, offers courses and workshops for the general public and clinical training for health professionals in practices including guided visualization and imagery, self-healing methods, mindfulness, dreamwork, and more. Learn more about AIMI by visiting www.drjerryepstein.org or emailing: mentalimageryinstitute@gmail.com.

www.ingramcontent.com/pod-product-compliance
Lightning Source LLC
Chambersburg PA
CBHW040241130526
44590CB00049B/4148